I0814425

NOT SO NEUROTYPICAL

The authorised representative in the EEA is Simon and Schuster Netherlands BV, Herculesplein 96 3584 AA Utrecht, Netherlands. (info@simonandschuster.nl)

Andrews McMeel Publishing
a division of Andrews McMeel Universal
1130 Walnut Street, Kansas City, Missouri 64106

www.andrewsmcmeel.com

26 27 28 29 30 RLP 10 9 8 7 6 5 4 3 2 1

ISBN: 979-8-8816-0550-6

Library of Congress Control Number: 2025940387

Editor: Erinn Pascal
Art Director: Jessica Rodriguez
Production Editor: Brianna Westervelt
Production Manager: Chadd Keim

ATTENTION: SCHOOLS AND BUSINESSES
Andrews McMeel books are available at quantity discounts with bulk purchase for educational, business, or sales promotional use. For information, please email the Andrews McMeel Publishing Special Sales Department: sales@andrewsmcmeel.com.

NOT SO NEUROTYPICAL

A FUN AND ILLUSTRATED CELEBRATION OF
30 INFLUENTIAL PEOPLE WITH ADHD

WORDS BY TERRANCE CRAWFORD

ART BY RACHEL CASH

Andrews McMeel
PUBLISHING®

TABLE OF CONTENTS

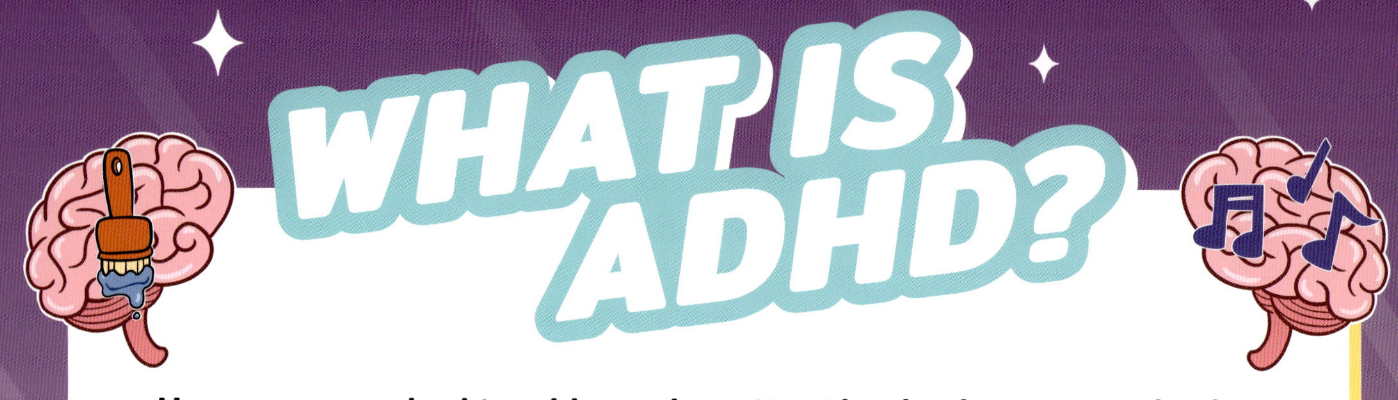

WHAT IS ADHD?

Have you ever had trouble paying attention in class, remembering instructions, or sitting still when you're supposed to? Everyone struggles with these things sometimes, but for kids with ADHD (that stands for attention deficit hyperactivity disorder), these challenges happen a *lot* more often.

ADHD isn't a bad thing—it just means the brain works a little differently. People with ADHD think, learn, and experience the world in unique ways, like:

FAST AND CREATIVE THINKING

Kids with ADHD often have super creative brains that work quickly—but that can sometimes make it tricky to focus on just one thing.

LOTS OF MOVEMENT

They might tap their fingers, wiggle in their seat, or always be on the go.

BIG ENERGY, BIG FEELINGS

They can also feel emotions in a BIG way—whether it's excitement, frustration, or joy.

ADHD brains often have a harder time keeping track of things, even when they're trying really hard!

Did you know there are three different kinds of ADHD?

- **Hyperactive ADHD:** Lots of energy and movement
- **Inattentive ADHD:** More daydreamy, but not as fidgety
- **Combined ADHD:** A little bit of both

ADHD brains are "**neurodiverse**," meaning they aren't how brains typically function.

No two people with ADHD are exactly the same, and that's what makes it so interesting!

In this book, you'll meet **30 incredible people** with ADHD—inventors, artists, athletes, and more—who didn't just succeed with ADHD . . . they thrived because of it!

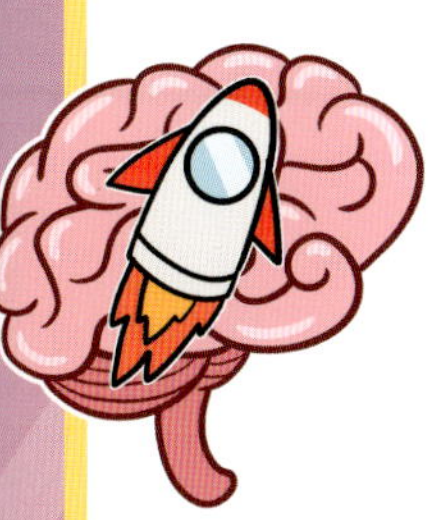

SO WHAT ARE YOU WAITING FOR? LET'S TURN THE PAGE AND GET STARTED!

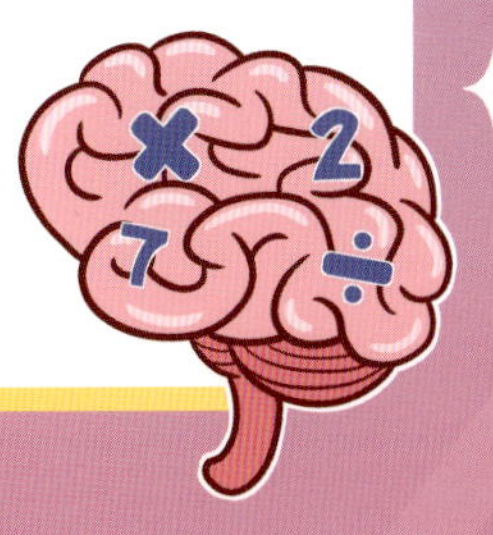

ADHD: A BRIEF HISTORY

THE MESOZOIC ERA

Lasted roughly 150 million years until an extinction event, likely an asteroid, wiped out most non-flying dinos.

We have no confirmed cases of ADHD from this time period, but it (could've) happened.

28,000 BCE (BEFORE COMMON ERA)

Homo sapiens, or modern-day humans, replaced Neanderthals as the dominant life-form on Earth. This was a controversial decision, as we have no record of Neanderthals doing homework or chores, but modern-day humans do. Neanderthals (probably) didn't have ADHD, but we can't confirm nor deny.

1798 CE (COMMON ERA)

A Scottish doctor named Sir Alexander Crichton wrote about what he called "the disease of attention," the condition that would come to be known as ADHD.

1902

Sir George Fredric Still, a British pediatrician, gave a series of lectures in which he described a condition in children characterized by "an abnormal defect of moral control," noting fifteen cases in boys and five in girls. Today, boys are significantly more likely to be diagnosed with ADHD than girls during childhood.

1968

The American Psychiatric Association's (APA) *Diagnostic and Statistical Manual of Mental Disorders*, or *DSM*, officially added "hyperkinetic reaction of childhood" to its diagnosis list.

1980S

The *DSM* was revised, and the "hyperkinetic reaction of childhood" was changed to "attention deficit disorder with or without hyperactivity"—essentially, what we now know today as attentive or inattentive ADHD.

1994

The APA revised the definition of ADHD to also include combined ADHD and added that symptoms can (and do) continue into adulthood.

PRESENT DAY

According to the United States Centers for Disease Control and Prevention, as of 2022, an estimated seven million American children have been diagnosed with ADHD—roughly 11.4 percent of kids.

2149

Who knows? This is a book about ADHD, not psychic abilities.

GO! GO! GO

SPORTS

From Olympic gold medalists to superstar players, some of the best athletes in the world have ADHD! Their energy, creativity, and ability to think outside the box have helped them dominate their respective sports.

SIMONE BILES

BIRTHDAY: MARCH 14, 1997

BORN IN: COLUMBUS, OHIO

ZODIAC SIGN: PISCES

Simone Biles is one of the greatest gymnasts of all time. In fact, she has won more Olympic and World Championship medals than any other gymnast in history!

But her journey started in an unexpected place: a daycare field trip. When Simone was in elementary school, her class visited a gymnastics center, and she was instantly hooked. She started flipping, tumbling, and practicing right away.

When she was nine years old, Simone was diagnosed with ADHD. Some people thought this might hold her back, but Simone didn't see it that way. Instead of letting her diagnosis stop her, she used it to her advantage. Her ability to hyperfocus helped her perfect her routines, and her extra energy gave her the power to soar through the air.

Today, Simone is a gold medalist, recipient of the Presidential Medal of Freedom, and mental health advocate. Simone proves that ADHD can be a source for inspiration.

FUN FACT:

Win or lose, Simone always rewards herself with pepperoni pizza after competitions. It's a tradition that she started in order to treat herself, even if she didn't take home a medal!

MICHAEL PHELPS
BIRTHDAY: JUNE 30, 1985
BORN IN: BALTIMORE, MARYLAND
ZODIAC SIGN: CANCER
"I THINK GOALS SHOULD NEVER BE EASY. THEY SHOULD FORCE YOU TO WORK, EVEN IF THEY ARE UNCOMFORTABLE AT THE TIME."

When Olympic gold medalist Michael Phelps was nine years old, he was struggling to pay attention in class. That's when he was diagnosed with ADHD.

"I was told by one of his teachers that he couldn't focus on anything," his mother recalled to *ADDitude* magazine in 2024. She continued, "That just hit my heart. It made me want to prove everyone wrong. I knew that, if I collaborated with Michael, he could achieve anything he set his mind to. Whenever a teacher would say, 'Michael can't do this,' I'd counter with, 'Well, what are you doing to help him?'"

Michael's mom enrolled him in swimming lessons, and then helped him navigate schoolwork through swimming, i.e., asking him math questions about races.

Swimming brought Michael structure and discipline. By the time he was ten, Michael had already set a national record for his age group in the 100-meter butterfly, proving that even at a young age, he was ready to make a splash!

As of 2025, Michael is one of the most decorated Olympians in history with twenty-eight medals, twenty-three of which are gold!

FUN FACT:

Michael likes to listen to music before competing, and particularly likes music by Eminem, Afrojack, Steve Aoki, and Skrillex.

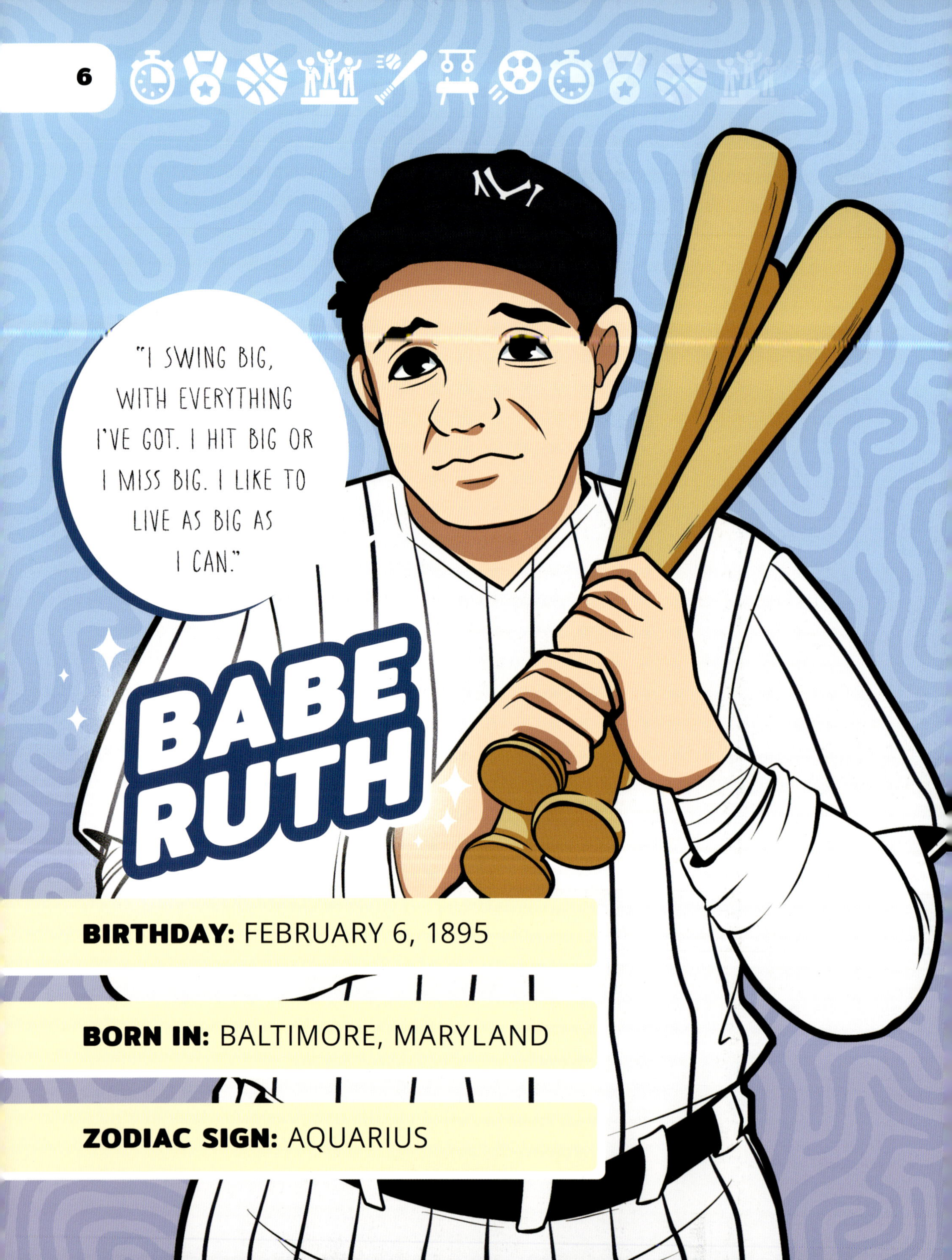

BIRTHDAY: FEBRUARY 6, 1895

BORN IN: BALTIMORE, MARYLAND

ZODIAC SIGN: AQUARIUS

Baseball legend George Herman Ruth Jr. (a.k.a. Babe Ruth) wasn't always a sports superstar. As a young child, Babe was full of energy. He was constantly running wild, getting into trouble, and often found himself in fights.

His parents struggled to keep up with him, so when he was just seven years old, they sent him to a boarding school called St. Mary's Industrial School for Boys. The school focused on discipline, learning trades, and playing sports—and it ended up changing Babe's life.

It was at St. Mary's that Babe discovered his love for baseball. Under the guidance of a kind coach named Brother Matthias, Babe practiced every chance he got. He learned to pitch, catch, and hit with incredible power. Soon, it was clear that he had a special talent, and he eventually became one of the most famous baseball players in history!

Although he was never officially diagnosed, some experts today believe that Babe's wild childhood behavior might have been caused by undiagnosed ADHD. Babe's ability to hyperfocus on baseball helped him become one of the greatest hitters the game has ever seen. He had 714 home runs during his career.

FUN FACT:

Although the Baby Ruth candy bar sounds like Babe's name, it's not actually named after him! The candy was coined for President Grover Cleveland's daughter, Ruth.

KEVIN GARNETT

BIRTHDAY: MAY 19, 1976

BORN IN: GREENVILLE, SOUTH CAROLINA

ZODIAC SIGN: TAURUS

Before winning an NBA Championship with the Boston Celtics, before being named to the All-Star team fifteen times, and before playing an incredible twenty-one seasons in the NBA . . . Kevin Garnett was just a kid who had a hard time focusing in school.

In his memoir, *KG: A to Z: An Uncensored Encyclopedia of Life, Basketball, and Everything in Between*, Kevin shared that he has ADHD and dyslexia (a learning disability that affects a person's ability to read and write).

But unlike some of his peers who were diagnosed in childhood, Kevin didn't make this discovery until he was an adult, and not until the very end of his basketball career. That meant he faced big challenges both on and off the court for most of his life without knowing exactly why learning and concentrating were so difficult for him.

But Kevin didn't let those challenges stop him. Instead, he used his intense focus, energy, and determination to chase his dreams—and slam dunk them! His passion for basketball, sharp instincts, and fierce attitude helped him become one of the greatest power forwards in NBA history.

FUN FACT:

Kevin's $126 million dollar deal with the Timberwolves was the largest deal in NBA history at the time (1998)!

TERRY BRADSHAW

BIRTHDAY: SEPTEMBER 2, 1948

BORN IN: SHREVEPORT, LOUISIANA

ZODIAC SIGN: VIRGO

Asked to describe himself as a child, Terry Bradshaw said that he was "rambunctious, never still, always in trouble, always dirty, never could keep my clothes clean, didn't even like to wear clothes . . . and then, of course, later on in life, you find out that you're an AD[H]D guy, so that helps explain why you weren't a good student."

If you recall from earlier, ADHD was first added to the *DSM* as a "hyper-kinetic reaction of childhood" in 1968—when Terry was already twenty years old!

But that didn't stop Terry. His racing mind and boundless energy turned out to be *exactly* what he needed on the football field. He worked hard, trained even harder, and eventually became the starting quarterback for the Pittsburgh Steelers.

In 1974, Terry led the Steelers to victory in Super Bowl IX, defeating the Minnesota Vikings. And that was just the beginning. He went on to win four Super Bowl titles, was named Super Bowl MVP twice, and earned a spot in the Pro Football Hall of Fame.

After retiring from football, Terry's big personality and quick wit made him a star on TV too. He became a longtime analyst and commentator on NFL broadcasts and even appeared in movies and TV shows, like *Modern Family* and *The Masked Singer*.

FUN FACT:

During his time as a quarterback for the Pittsburgh Steelers, Terry also recorded a series of country songs.

MUSIC

Have you ever found yourself tapping your toe to a beat in your head or drumming on your desk with your pencil during class? Like there's a rhythm playing in your head that's all your own?

For some musicians, that's how they feel all the time. From chart-topping pop stars to legendary composers, some of the most talented musicians in the world have ADHD! Their passion, creativity, and one-of-a-kind way of thinking have helped them write unforgettable songs, master instruments, and light up stages around the globe.

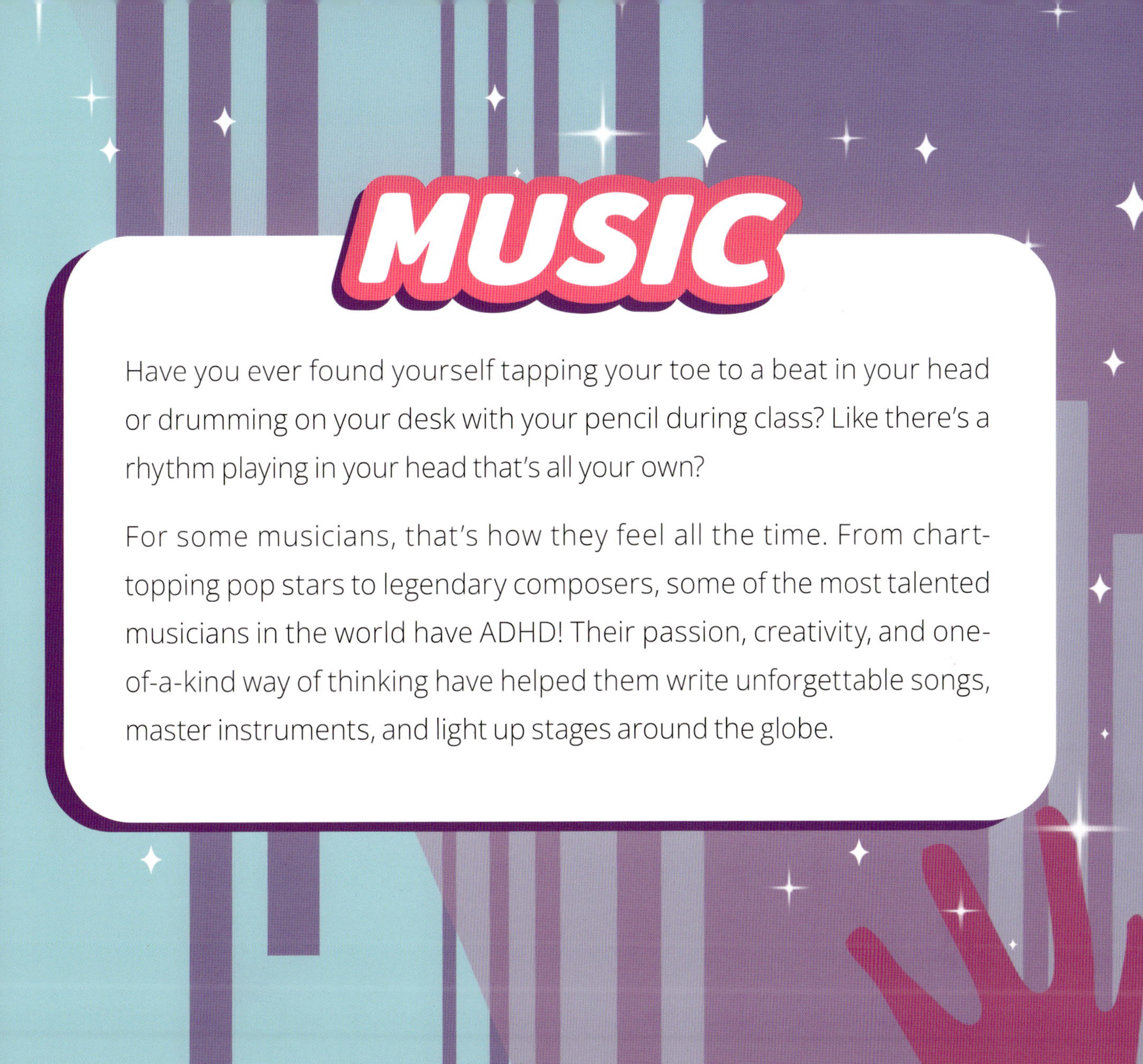

BIRTHDAY: MARCH 15, 1975

BORN IN: LOS ANGELES, CALIFORNIA

ZODIAC SIGN: PISCES

You might know will.i.am (born William James Adams Jr.) as a Grammy Award–winning producer, musician, and the founder of the chart-topping group The Black Eyed Peas. Did you know he's also an inventor, entrepreneur, fashion designer, and the founder of a foundation that helps provide education and technology to kids from low-income communities?

will.i.am is obviously a creative powerhouse. But how does he do it all?

According to will.i.am, part of the answer is ADHD. He's open about his diagnosis and how it affects his life and how music helps him channel his thoughts and energy in a positive way.

"One thing I learned about ADHD is that it's hard to keep your attention, and you can't sit still and you're always moving and thinking about a whole bunch of things. But those traits work well for me in studios and in meetings about creative ideas. It keeps my mind from wandering," he once said. "I can stay in the music. Music brings control to my thoughts."

FUN FACT:

will.i.am's diet is completely plant-based and he has been a vegan since 2017.

SOLANGE KNOWLES

BIRTHDAY: JUNE 24, 1986

BORN IN: HOUSTON, TEXAS

ZODIAC SIGN: CANCER

"I TRY TO TRANSITION MY ENERGY INTO JUST HAVING FUN."

FUN FACT:

Solange sang the theme song for the iconic Disney Channel series *The Proud Family*.

Solange Knowles is a Grammy Award–winning singer, songwriter, and artist who loves to make music that inspires people. She's known for hit songs like "Cranes in the Sky" and "Almeda" and even starred in the movie *Bring It On: All or Nothing*.

But Solange doesn't just make music. She also creates cool performances that mix dance, art, and storytelling.

In addition to being an artistic powerhouse, Solange is a proud advocate for Black culture. She celebrates natural hair, supports the Black Lives Matter movement, and uses her platform to uplift and empower others.

She's also a fashion icon, collaborating with brands like Puma, Gucci, and her family's clothing line, House of Deréon.

Solange was diagnosed with ADHD twice—she didn't believe it the first time and got a second opinion. Now, she speaks openly about mental health, showing the world that being different is something to embrace.

FUN FACT:

She is also Beyoncé's sister, but as Solange says, "I'm not her and never will be."

MOZART

BIRTHDAY: JANUARY 27, 1756

BORN IN: SALZBURG, AUSTRIA

ZODIAC SIGN: AQUARIUS

You've probably heard of Wolfgang Amadeus Mozart. He's one of the most famous musical geniuses in all of history. Even though he lived over 250 years ago, his symphonies, operas, and concertos are still performed all over the world today.

But did you know Mozart was also known for being super energetic, silly, and sometimes a little *wild*? His friend once said that he liked to jump up, leap over tables and chairs, meow like a cat, "and turn somersaults like an unruly boy."

While we can't know for sure, many psychiatric experts believe that Mozart may have had ADHD.

Even though he sometimes had trouble staying still or following the rules, Mozart used his incredible imagination and focus on music to compose hundreds of pieces by the time he was thirty-five!

FUN FACT:

Mozart loved playing practical jokes on people. He created a piece called "A Musical Joke" to make fun of those who he thought to be bad composers. The joke? All of the passages in "A Musical Joke" were played out of tune.

BIRTHDAY: OCTOBER 21, 1995

BORN IN: LOS ANGELES, CALIFORNIA

ZODIAC SIGN: LIBRA

Doja Cat (born Amala Ratna Zandile Dlamini) is a superstar singer, rapper, and performer known for her catchy songs, wild style, and totally original music videos.

With hits like "Say So," "Woman," and "Kiss Me More," she's topped the charts, won Grammys, and become one of the most creative voices in modern pop and hip-hop.

But before she was a global icon, Doja was a kid who loved dancing, drawing, and making music on her computer. She's talked openly about having ADHD and how it made school a challenge growing up.

"I have a really bad impulse control; I like to react to things really quick," she once said to a magazine.

Still, she didn't let that stop her. Instead, Doja pours her energy and imagination into creating. From making beats in her bedroom to going viral with her funny and clever videos, she turned her one-of-a-kind brain into a superpower.

Today, she's known for her bold fashion, unforgettable live performances, and being completely herself—whether she's designing a tour, starring in a music video, or performing on national TV.

FUN FACT:

Doja Cat is obsessed with Taco Bell's Mexican pizza and wrote a song about it. The line "Mexican pizza is the pizza for you and me!" was inspired by the "Krusty Krab Pizza" song in *SpongeBob SquarePants*.

JUSTIN BIEBER

BIRTHDAY: MARCH 1, 1994

BORN IN: LONDON, ONTARIO, CANADA

ZODIAC SIGN: PISCES

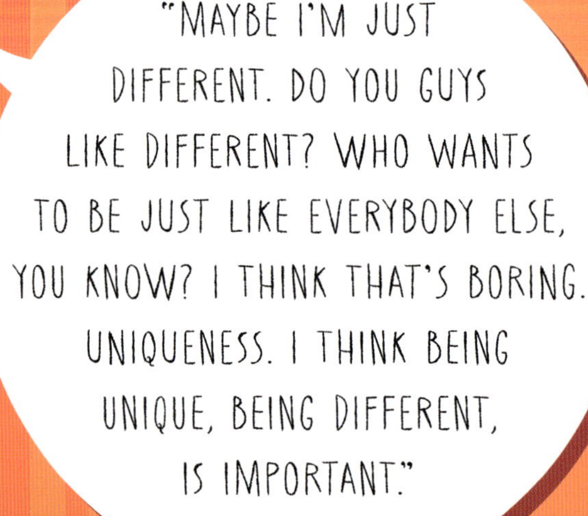

Before he was a global pop star, Justin Bieber was just a kid in Canada with a big love for music. He taught himself to play the guitar, drums, piano, and trumpet, and started singing for fun around his hometown.

Justin's mom, Pattie, posted videos of him performing on YouTube, and those clips changed his life forever when a music manager discovered him online. Soon after, Justin was signed to a record label.

At just fifteen years old, Justin released his first hit single, "One Time," and became a teen sensation almost overnight. Since then, he's grown into one of the bestselling music artists of all time, with hits like "Baby," "Sorry," "Love Yourself," and "Peaches."

Justin has been open about living with ADHD and how it affects him. He's talked about how taking medication helps, but also how it can impact his mental health. By speaking out, he's helped others feel less alone and reminded fans that it's okay to ask for help.

Today, Justin continues to make music, support mental health awareness, and inspire millions of fans with his honesty and heart.

FUN FACT:

Justin can solve a Rubik's Cube in under two minutes—talk about brainpower!

BENNY BLANCO

BIRTHDAY: MARCH 8, 1988

BORN IN: RESTON, VIRGINIA

ZODIAC SIGN: PISCES

You might not see Benny Blanco (born Benjamin Joseph Levin) on stage singing every night, but chances are, you've heard his work!

Benny is one of the most successful music producers and songwriters in the world. He's helped create hit songs for artists like Katy Perry, Ed Sheeran, Rihanna, Selena Gomez, Addison Rae, Gracie Abrams, and Halsey, just to name a few.

Benny has been open about living with ADHD and how it made school a struggle for him when he was a kid. But instead of giving up, he leaned into his creativity—and that's where he found his rhythm.

Music gave him a way to focus, express himself, and turn his big ideas into award-winning songs. Today, he's earned multiple Grammy nominations, produced dozens of No. 1 hits, and even written a cookbook!

FUN FACT:

Benny once played a teddy bear in his partner Selena Gomez's music video.

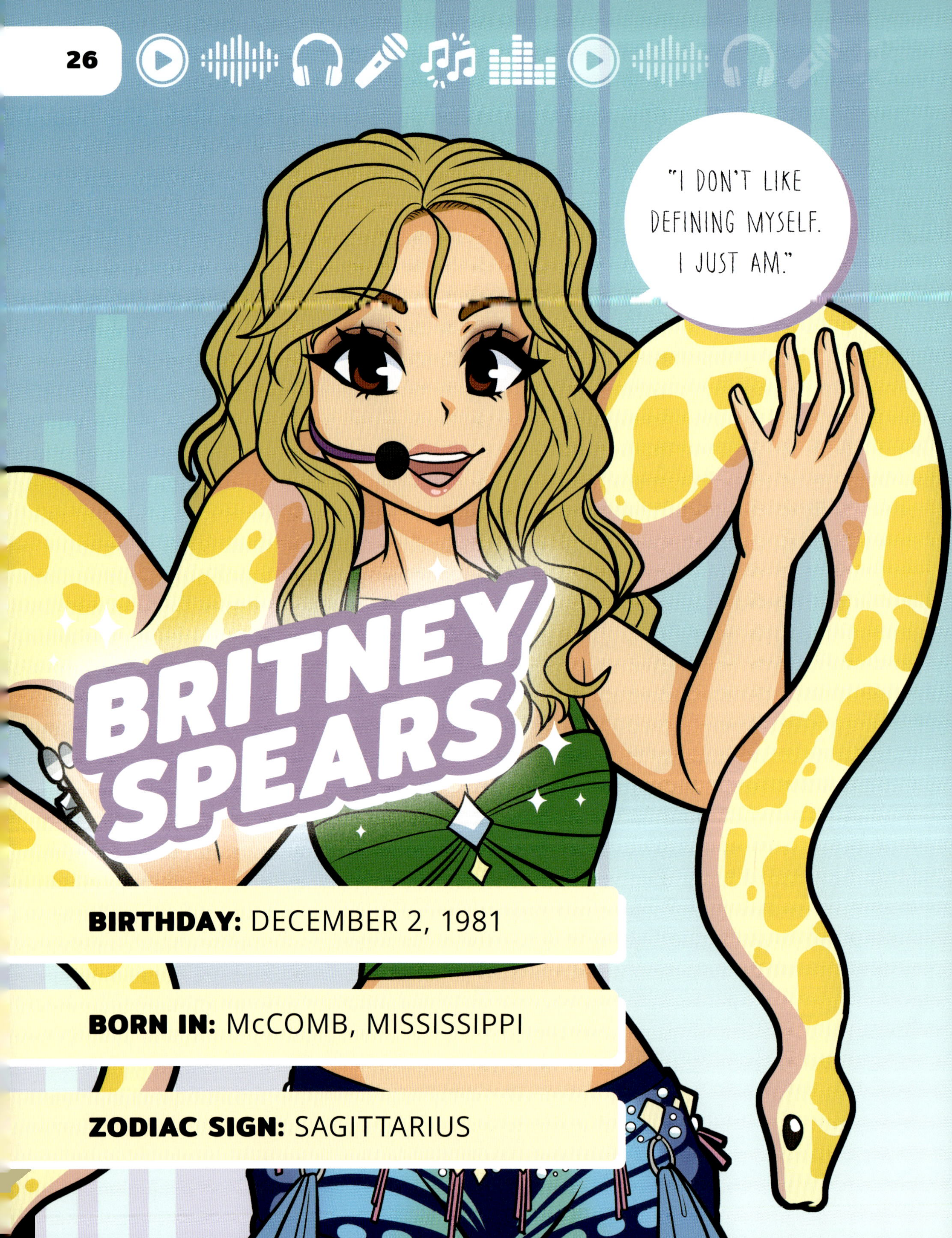

BRITNEY SPEARS

BIRTHDAY: DECEMBER 2, 1981

BORN IN: McCOMB, MISSISSIPPI

ZODIAC SIGN: SAGITTARIUS

Before she became a global superstar and *New York Times* best-selling author, Britney Spears was just a small-town girl with a huge voice. She got her start singing and dancing on *The All-New Mickey Mouse Club*, and soon after, rocketed to fame with hit songs like "...Baby One More Time" and "Toxic."

With over 150 million records sold worldwide, Britney is one of the bestselling pop artists of all time, and a true icon of the music industry.

But what many fans might not know is that Britney was diagnosed with ADHD as a teenager. She has shared that it can make it hard for her to focus and stay still, especially during long rehearsals or performances.

To help, Britney mixes up her dance moves and workouts to keep things exciting and avoid getting bored.

Britney proves that with the right coping strategy, we can all be "stronger than yesterday!"

FUN FACT:

In 1992, ten-year-old Britney was the understudy for future Broadway star Laura Bell Bundy in the off-Broadway musical *Ruthless!* She performed with the show for eight months, but eventually stepped away, saying the repetition started to bore her. Her replacement? None other than future movie star Natalie Portman!

NICKI MINAJ

BIRTHDAY: DECEMBER 8, 1982

BORN IN: SAINT JAMES, PORT OF SPAIN, TRINIDAD AND TOBAGO

ZODIAC SIGN: SAGITTARIUS

"MAYBE YOUR WEIRD IS MY NORMAL. WHO'S TO SAY?"

Nicki Minaj (born Onika Tanya Maraj) wasn't always one of the biggest names in rap. Born in Trinidad and raised in Queens, New York, Nicki faced a tough childhood and often escaped into her imagination. That creativity led her to invent new characters and eventually adopt the name Nicki Minaj. She wrote her first rap at just twelve years old!

After being discovered on a social media website by rapper Lil Wayne, Nicki rose to fame with her bold style, quick flow, and unforgettable lyrics.

"I have a difficult time getting out what I have to say," Nicki once posted on social media. She has spoken about living with ADHD, which can sometimes make it hard to stay focused or organized. But she's also shared that her nonstop energy, creative thinking, and ability to juggle multiple ideas at once have been superpowers in her career.

Nicki had one of the top ten highest-grossing rap tours of all time, and she's the first female rapper to have over 100 entries on the Billboard Hot 100 chart. She's also won dozens of awards and collaborated with some of the biggest names in music.

Today, Nicki continues to break records, release new music, and inspire fans around the world, all while being a proud mom and entrepreneur.

FUN FACT:

When Nicki is on tour, she travels with several stuffed animals. She once lost her pink stuffed monkey, Oscar, at the airport and offered up a $50,000 reward to anyone who could find him.

TYLER, THE CREATOR

BIRTHDAY: MARCH 6, 1991

BORN IN: HAWTHORNE, CALIFORNIA

ZODIAC SIGN: PISCES

"I SUFFER FROM ADHD, I SHOULD WIN A[N] AWARD FOR BEING ME."

Rapper. Filmmaker. Fashion designer.

How does Tyler, the Creator find time to be a multi-hyphenate and run his own record label?

Well, the California-born artist, whose real name is Tyler Gregory Okonma, has built an empire out of pure creativity. He's known for his wild imagination, bold ideas, and genre-defying music.

Tyler has gone back and forth in interviews and lyrics about whether he has ADHD, but he's admitted to relating to the symptoms, like racing thoughts, bouncing between interests, and constantly needing to create something new. But rather than slowing him down, those traits have helped him build a one-of-a-kind career.

He's the founder of the influential collective Odd Future, the creator of his own fashion brand GOLF le FLEUR*, and the winner of multiple Grammys. His albums *IGOR* and *Call Me If You Get Lost* both debuted at No. 1, and he's directed his own music videos and even his own TV show.

Today, Tyler continues to push boundaries in music, fashion, and beyond—all while staying 100 percent himself. He also has asthma and has been seen on stage with an inhaler.

FUN FACT:

Tyler is a massive fan of skateboarding and he frequently references skate culture in his music and fashion.

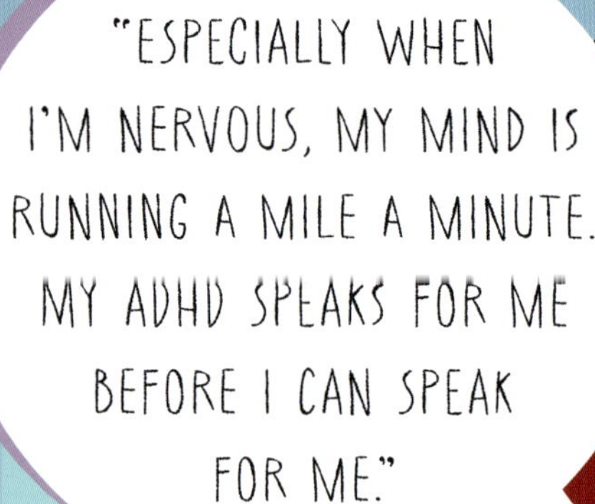

BIRTHDAY: NOVEMBER 8, 1989

BORN IN: ST. LOUIS, MISSOURI

ZODIAC SIGN: SCORPIO

Born Solána Imani Rowe, Grammy Award–winning singer and songwriter SZA is known for her soulful voice, honest lyrics, and dreamy sound. But behind the music, she's also been open about her struggles with ADHD.

On X (formerly Twitter), SZA has shared how the condition impacts her creativity, sometimes making it tough to focus or finish songs, depending on whether she's taking medication.

Despite the challenges, SZA has found her rhythm. Her debut album *Ctrl* was a massive hit and earned her multiple Grammy nominations. Her follow-up album *SOS* debuted at No. 1 on the Billboard 200 and stayed there for ten nonconsecutive weeks, making music history!

Today, SZA continues to break records, sell out arenas, and inspire fans with her vulnerability, talent, and one-of-a-kind voice. Lucky for all of us, she's still having her "Good Days"!

FUN FACT:

Before she was a Grammy Award–winning artist, SZA was a gymnast for thirteen years. As a sophomore in high school, she was the fifth-ranked gymnast in the US, according to her.

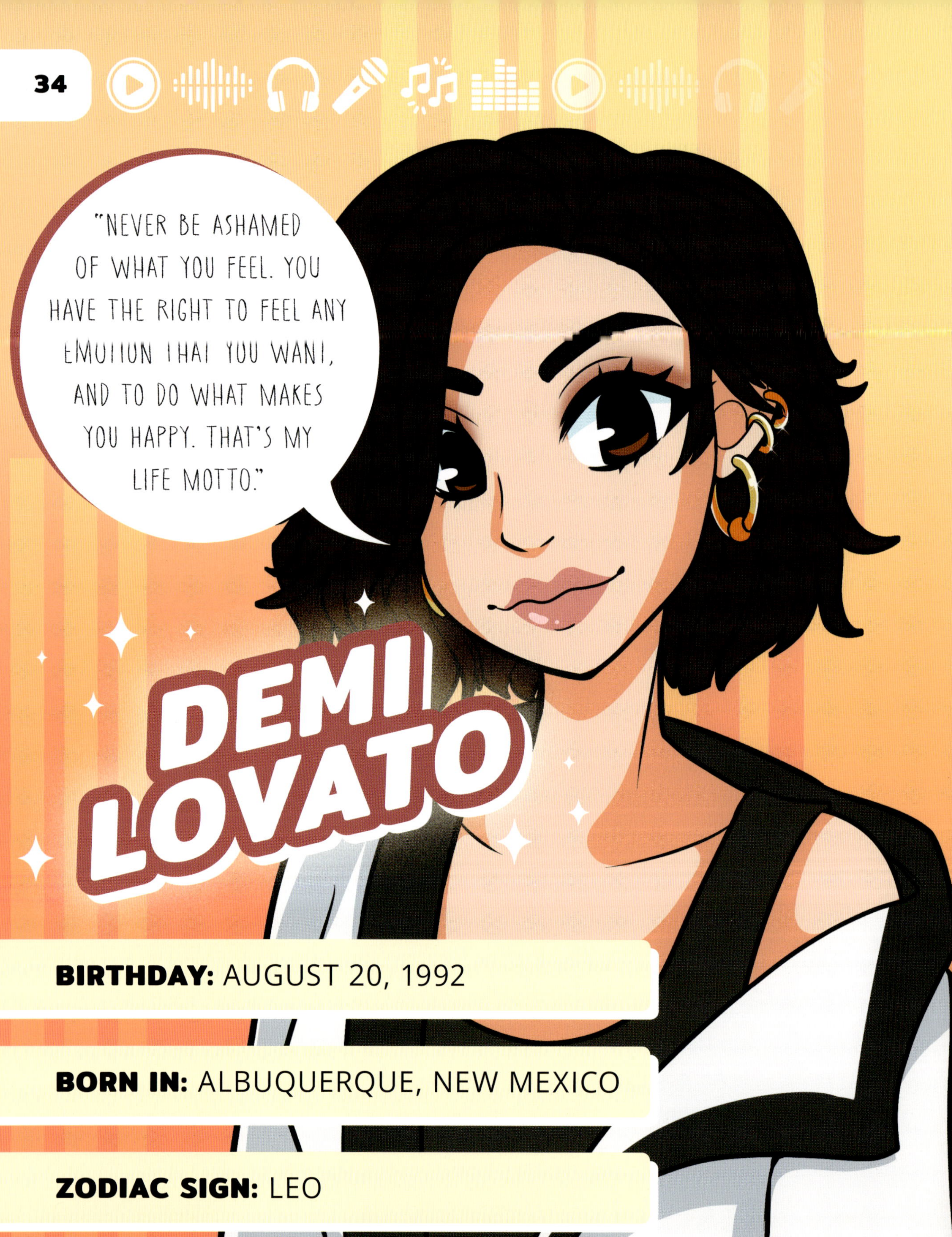

DEMI LOVATO

BIRTHDAY: AUGUST 20, 1992

BORN IN: ALBUQUERQUE, NEW MEXICO

ZODIAC SIGN: LEO

Demi Lovato (short for Demetria Devonne Lovato) wasn't always the superstar we know today.

Born in Albuquerque, New Mexico, and raised in Dallas, Texas, Demi faced many challenges growing up. She found solace in performing, starting her career as a child actress on *Barney & Friends*. Demi's creativity and talent led her to Disney Channel, where she starred in the hit movie *Camp Rock* and TV show *Sonny with a Chance*.

Demi's journey to fame wasn't easy. She released her first album, *Don't Forget*, at just sixteen years old, and her powerful voice quickly made her a pop sensation.

But Demi has also been open about living with ADHD; she first shared her diagnosis in 2021, in her docuseries, *Child Star*. She's shared that while ADHD presents challenges, it also fuels her creativity and energy, helping her juggle multiple projects at once.

Today, Demi has been nominated for Grammys, written a *New York Times* bestselling book, and became a vocal advocate for mental health. Demi has shown that with determination and self-belief, you can overcome any obstacle. Demi continues to inspire fans around the world through music, acting, and advocacy.

FUN FACT:

Demi is obsessed with the movie *Mean Girls* and can quote every word of it.

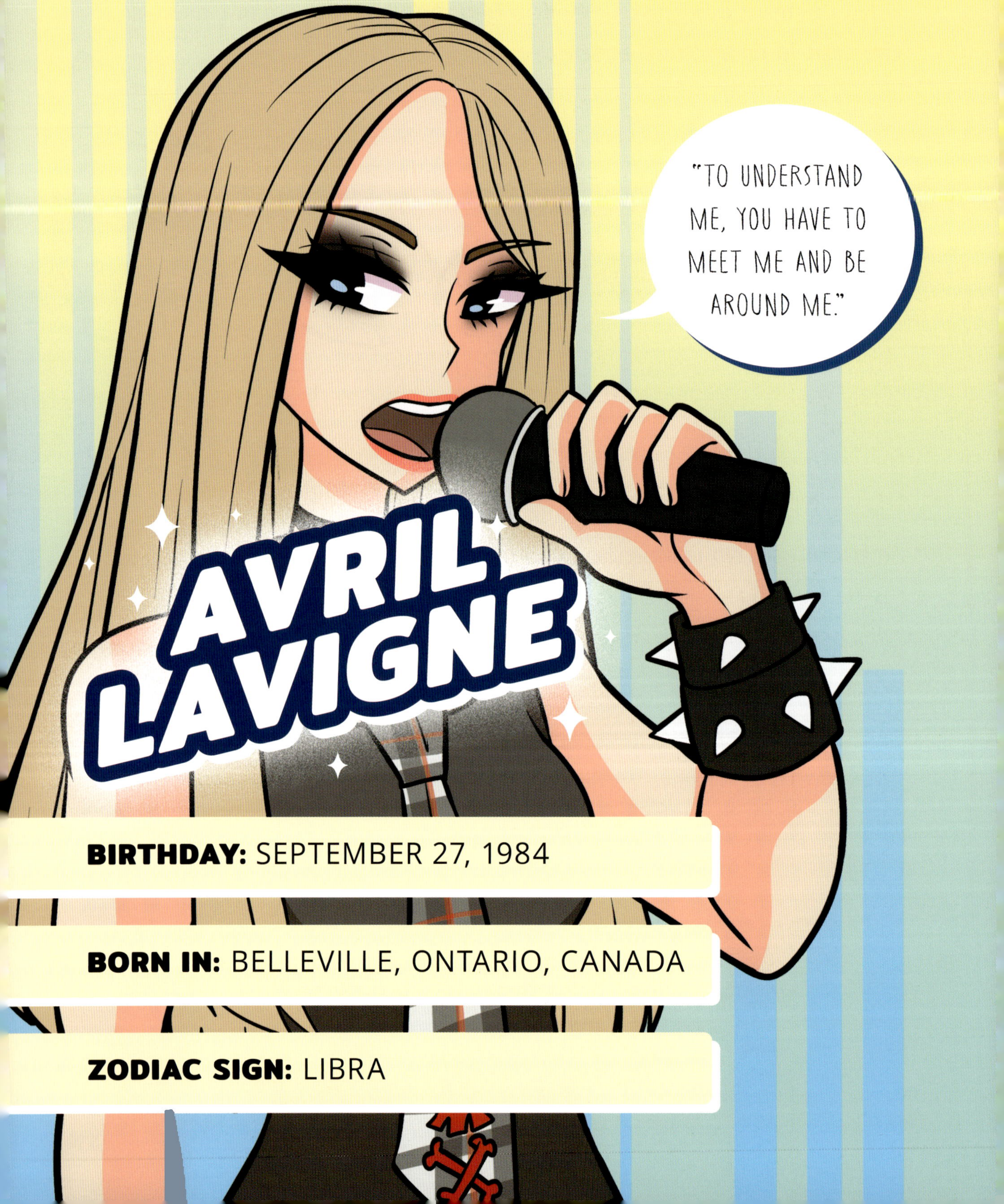

"TO UNDERSTAND ME, YOU HAVE TO MEET ME AND BE AROUND ME."

AVRIL LAVIGNE

BIRTHDAY: SEPTEMBER 27, 1984

BORN IN: BELLEVILLE, ONTARIO, CANADA

ZODIAC SIGN: LIBRA

Avril Ramona Lavigne, Canada's pop punk princess, grew up in Ontario. Diagnosed with ADHD in elementary school, Avril often found herself in trouble for misbehaving or starting fights. Her parents tried various activities to channel her energy, including playing hockey on the boys' team. But it wasn't until her dad transformed their basement into a music studio, complete with a drum kit, microphone, keyboard, and guitars, that Avril found her true passion.

Avril's debut album, *Let Go*, became the bestselling album of the twenty-first century by a Canadian artist, featuring hits like "Complicated" and "Sk8er Boi."

As of 2025, Avril has been nominated for eight Grammys and has sold over forty million albums worldwide.

Beyond music, Avril has ventured into acting, with roles in films like *Over the Hedge* and *Fast Food Nation*. She's also a philanthropist, founding The Avril Lavigne Foundation to support individuals with serious illnesses and disabilities.

Avril's journey shows that with the right support and determination, you can turn challenges into strengths. Nothing "complicated" about that!

FUN FACT:

Avril recorded the chorus of her song "Girlfriend" in eight different languages: English, Mandarin, Japanese, Spanish, French, German, Italian, and Portuguese!

HOLLYWOOD

Does your brain ever feel like it's popping off a million ideas a minute, lighting up like the flashbulbs of cameras on the red carpet? You're not alone. Dozens of movie and TV stars feel the same way when their ADHD symptoms rear their heads.

But that's part of their magic. ADHD didn't stop these people from becoming stars—it helped them to stand out.

EMMA WATSON

BIRTHDAY: APRIL 15, 1990

BORN IN: PARIS, FRANCE

ZODIAC SIGN: ARIES

"IF YOU TRULY POUR YOUR HEART INTO WHAT YOU BELIEVE IN, EVEN IF IT MAKES YOU VULNERABLE, AMAZING THINGS CAN AND WILL HAPPEN."

Emma Watson is not just known for her iconic role as Hermione Granger in the *Harry Potter* films, or as live-action Belle in Disney's *Beauty and the Beast*; she's also a brilliant advocate for gender equality and a UN Women Goodwill Ambassador!

Born in Paris, France, and raised in England, Emma grew up on screen, enchanting audiences with her intelligence and bravery. And, according to an article in *ADDitude* magazine, she has ADHD, too.

Emma's accomplishments go beyond acting. She graduated from Brown University with a degree in English literature, proving she's just as dedicated to her education as Hermione! Additionally, as a UN Women's goodwill ambassador, Emma launched the HeForShe campaign, encouraging everyone to join the fight for gender equality.

Emma's journey shows that with determination and support, you can achieve great things, no matter the challenges. She continues to inspire fans around the world with her talent, intelligence, and advocacy. Way to go, Emma!

Emma is a certified yoga and meditation instructor.

MARK
RUFFALO
BIRTHDAY: NOVEMBER 22, 1967
BORN IN: KENOSHA, WISCONSIN
ZODIAC SIGN: SAGITTARIUS
"DON'T LOSE YOUR HEART, JUST KEEP GOING, KEEP AT IT."

Mark Ruffalo isn't just an amazing actor. You might know him best as Bruce Banner, a.k.a. the Hulk, in Marvel movies like *The Avengers* and *Thor: Ragnarok*. But he's also somewhat of a superhero in real life!

Born in Kenosha, Wisconsin, Mark grew up with undiagnosed dyslexia and ADHD.

Despite the challenges of ADHD, which can make it hard to focus and stay organized, Mark has used his creativity and energy to become a successful actor. He's shared that his ADHD helps him think outside the box and bring unique ideas to his roles.

Beyond acting, Mark is a dedicated environmental activist, fighting for clean energy and against climate change. He's also a loving dad to three kids and enjoys spending time with his family. He even has a star on the Hollywood Walk of Fame!

FUN FACT:

Mark has had many cats, including: Inky, Biscotti, Felix, Magnus, and Hansel.

TREVOR NOAH

BIRTHDAY: FEBRUARY 20, 1984

BORN IN: JOHANNESBURG, TRANSVAAL (NOW GAUTENG), SOUTH AFRICA

ZODIAC SIGN: PISCES

Trevor Noah is an award-winning TV host, comedian, and author. He's perhaps best known for hosting *The Daily Show*, a popular late-night talk show on Comedy Central, from 2015 to 2022.

Growing up, Trevor moved around a lot and often felt like an outsider. But he discovered that his humor—making people laugh—was his ticket to fitting in and making friends.

Trevor was diagnosed with ADHD as an adult after struggling with focus, impulsivity, and a restless mind for years. This diagnosis was a turning point for him, as he realized that what he had previously seen as personal shortcomings were actually symptoms of ADHD.

Trevor's sharp wit and insightful commentary made him a favorite among viewers. Today, he is open about his ADHD diagnosis and uses his platform to raise awareness about neurodiversity. He continues to inspire people with his comedy, stories, and positive attitude.

FUN FACT:

According to IMDb, Trevor speaks English, Xhosa, Zulu, Sotho, Tswana, Tsonga, Afrikaans, and some German.

GRETA GERWIG

BIRTHDAY: AUGUST 4, 1983

BORN IN: SACRAMENTO, CALIFORNIA

ZODIAC SIGN: LEO

"COURAGE DOESN'T GROW OVERNIGHT. IT CAN BE A LONG PROCESS."

Director Greta Gerwig is known for the super popular films *Barbie, Lady Bird,* and *Little Women*. But she wasn't always a hugely successful Hollywood director.

Greta was an avid reader as a child. She loved books so much that she would often read at the dinner table, even though it was against the rules.

At school, Greta was a "real rule follower" and had a tremendous amount of enthusiasm.

She once said, "I was just interested in, like, everything. I had a really active imagination. I had a lot of really deep feelings. I was emotional." These deep feelings and her active imagination have certainly helped her achieve great things!

Greta was diagnosed with ADHD as an adult, which helped her understand her boundless energy and enthusiasm. She's shared that her ADHD helps her think outside the box and bring unique ideas to her work.

FUN FACT:

One of Greta's hobbies growing up was fencing, but she had to give it up due to its hefty price tag. She also tried ballet but realized it wasn't for her.

JIM CARREY

BIRTHDAY: JANUARY 17, 1962

BORN IN: NEWMARKET, ONTARIO, CANADA

ZODIAC SIGN: CAPRICORN

"MY REPORT CARD ALWAYS JUST SAID, 'JIM FINISHES FIRST AND THEN DISRUPTS THE OTHER STUDENTS.'"

Before he became one of the highest-paid comic actors of his time, Jim Carrey's life wasn't all jokes and laughter. Perhaps you know him as the Grinch in *How the Grinch Stole Christmas*, Count Olaf in *A Series of Unfortunate Events*, or his fantastic portrayal of Dr. Robotnik himself, the Eggman, in the *Sonic the Hedgehog* films.

Born in Canada, Jim went through a tough adolescence, even experiencing homelessness before he got his big break. At age fifteen, Jim found work as a janitor to support his struggling family.

Jim found solace in front of mirrors, practicing the funny faces that would later make him millions. He discovered his talent for comedy and, as a teenager, began doing stand-up, leading him down the path to become one of the world's favorite funny men.

Jim was diagnosed with ADHD later in life, after struggling with focus, impulsivity, and a restless mind for years.

FUN FACT:

When Jim was a child, his mother was very sick, and he would do anything to make her laugh, including wearing tap shoes to bed so if she woke up in the middle of the night he could make her smile.

LISA LING

BIRTHDAY: AUGUST 30, 1973

BORN IN: SACRAMENTO, CALIFORNIA

ZODIAC SIGN: VIRGO

"TRY TO ACCOMPLISH THINGS YOU HAVE ALWAYS DREAMT OF WHILE YOU CAN. I KNOW IT SOUNDS CLICHÉ, BUT THE BIGGEST LESSON I HAVE LEARNED IS THAT LIFE IS PRECIOUS; ENJOY IT WHILE IT LASTS."

Lisa Ling is a journalist and TV host who uses her curiosity and energy to explore important stories around the world. She's been a journalist for CNN and Channel One News, a cohost on *The View*, the host of *National Geographic Explorer*, and even a special correspondent for *The Oprah Winfrey Show*.

Lisa's endless questions and love for storytelling became her greatest strengths.

When Lisa was doing a report on ADHD in 2014, she realized that she had many of the symptoms. Lisa was forty when she got the official diagnosis and says she didn't recognize it until then as she wasn't hyperactive.

But Lisa was always a bit inattentive. She recalled, "I could go through an entire period and not retain a sentence if I [wasn't] interested in the topic or in the subject matter."

Now, Lisa makes sure to give herself quiet time each day to help her mind focus. She's said of her ADHD, "In a strange way, I do feel like it has helped me. I can hyperfocus on things that I am excited and passionate about."

FUN FACT:

Lisa volunteers at animal sanctuaries like The Gentle Barn.

HOWIE MANDEL

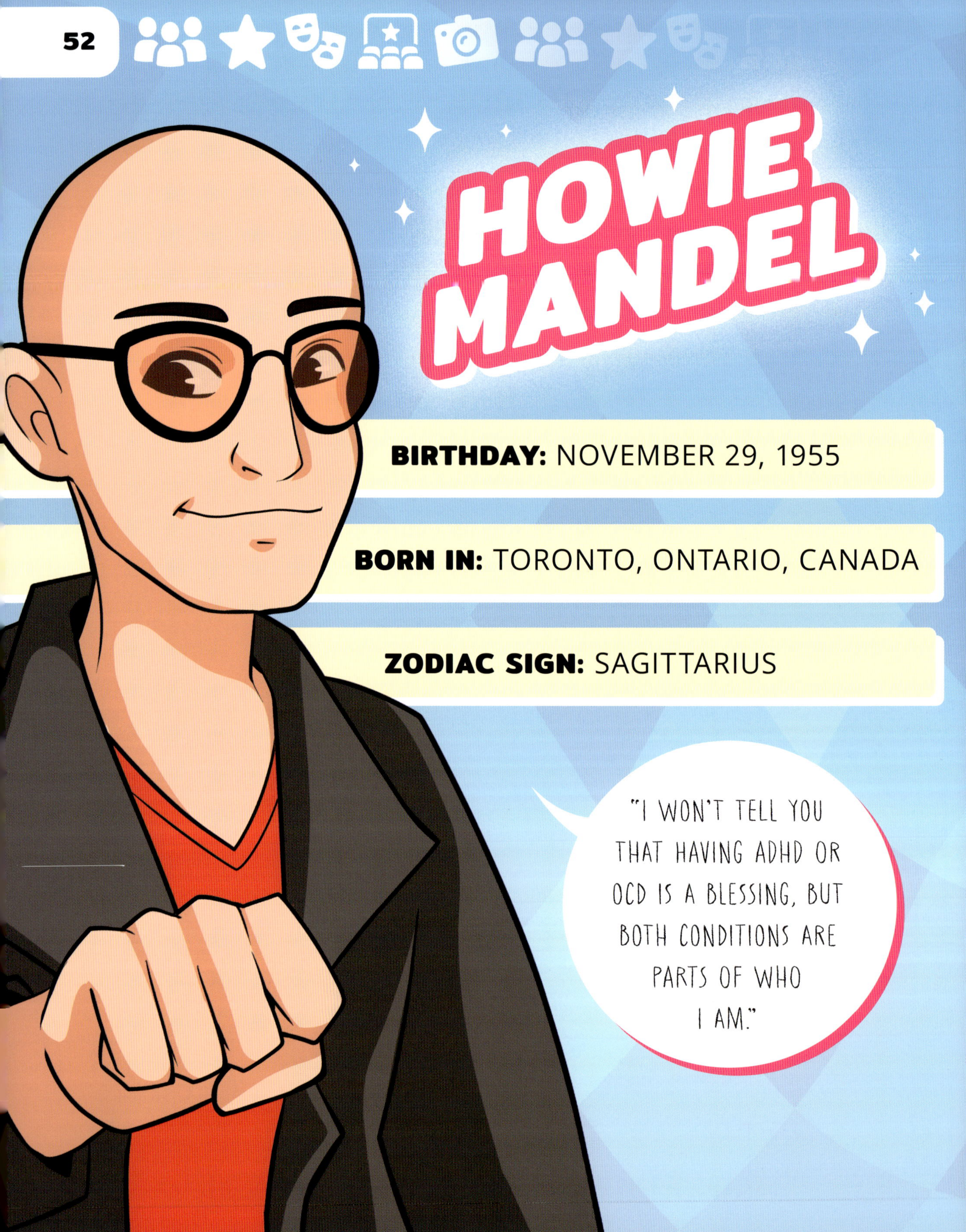

BIRTHDAY: NOVEMBER 29, 1955

BORN IN: TORONTO, ONTARIO, CANADA

ZODIAC SIGN: SAGITTARIUS

When Howie Mandel was a kid, sitting still and following the rules wasn't exactly his thing. He was always full of energy, cracking jokes, and pulling pranks—sometimes getting into trouble for it. But that same playful, fast-thinking brain helped him become a famous comedian, actor, and TV host.

You might know him from *America's Got Talent*, *Canada's Got Talent*, *Deal or No Deal*, or as the voice of Bobby in *Bobby's World*. He is also an investor and big fan of technology, as well as an influential advocate for mental health.

In addition to having ADHD, Howie also has obsessive-compulsive disorder, or OCD.

He is very active in the ADHD and OCD awareness communities, and passionate about platforming awareness for them.

FUN FACT:

Howie has stars on both the Hollywood Walk of Fame and Canada's Walk of Fame.

RENEÉ RAPP

BIRTHDAY: JANUARY 10, 2000

BORN IN: HUNTERSVILLE, NORTH CAROLINA

ZODIAC SIGN: CAPRICORN

"I DIDN'T KNOW OR UNDERSTAND WHAT [ADHD] WAS, BUT NOW I DO AND I REALLY LOVE IT. I THINK IT HELPS ME A LOT."

Reneé Rapp is a singer and actress who shows that ADHD is just part of what makes her shine.

Growing up in North Carolina, she channeled her energy into performing, landing the role of Regina George on Broadway in *Mean Girls: The Musical* and later releasing heartfelt songs like "Too Well."

She later reprised the role of Regina George in the 2024 movie adaptation of the musical, which skyrocketed her to even more fame!

Also that year, Reneé came out as a lesbian. She's outspoken about LGBTQ+ issues as well as mental health.

In May 2025, Reneé performed her lead single "Leave Me Alone" at the American Music Awards.

Whether she's on stage or in the studio, Reneé proves that success comes from being yourself and following what you love.

FUN FACT:

Reneé played varsity golf in high school.

RYAN GOSLING

BIRTHDAY: NOVEMBER 12, 1980

BORN IN: LONDON, ONTARIO, CANADA

ZODIAC SIGN: SCORPIO

Ryan Gosling was born to working-class parents in Ontario, Canada.

Growing up, he had difficulty reading, which led to bullying. His mom decided to homeschool him and encouraged him to explore his passions: performing and acting.

Ryan began participating in talent shows alongside his sister and in dance competitions. When he was twelve, he successfully auditioned for a role on *The All-New Mickey Mouse Club*, joining a cast that included future music stars Britney Spears, Christina Aguilera, and Justin Timberlake.

He went on to star in iconic films like *The Notebook*, *Barbie*, and *Blade Runner 2049*.

Ryan's journey shows that with support and determination, you can turn challenges into strengths. He continues to inspire fans with his talent and positive attitude.

Ryan was *this* close to becoming a Backstreet Boy when he and original BSB member AJ McLean lived in the same New York City building. As the Backstreet Boys raced up the charts, Ryan tried to get back in touch with his old friend. "They're not returning my calls. I try not to think about it," he joked.

CHANGEMAKERS

Some of the most creative and successful people in the world have ADHD, turning it into a tool to work for them. Read on to meet amazing authors, powerful politicians, and business owners who just may inspire you to push past what you think is possible.

DAV PILKEY
BIRTHDAY: MARCH 4, 1966
BORN IN: CLEVELAND, OHIO
ZODIAC SIGN: PISCES
"MY ADHD HELPED ME TO WRITE STORIES THAT WERE NOT BORING."
NEW YORK TIMES BESTSELLING AUTHOR

Dav Pilkey, the creator of *Captain Underpants* and *Dog Man*, shows that ADHD can be a conduit for creativity.

As a kid, Dav had a tough time sitting still or paying attention in class, and his ADHD often got him into trouble. But instead of giving up, he used his imagination to dream up funny stories and silly characters.

Diagnosed with ADHD and dyslexia in second grade, Dav's hyperactivity often got him sent out of the classroom. He used that time to work on his drawing and storytelling, creating the beloved characters Captain Underpants and Dog Man. His books have become bestsellers, making millions of kids laugh and love reading.

Dav's journey shows that ADHD isn't a problem—it's just a different way of thinking that can spark big ideas! He's also won numerous awards, including the Caldecott Honor for his book *The Paperboy*.

Dav continues to inspire kids with his creativity and positive attitude.

FUN FACT:

Dav has a four-inch-long Japanese rhinoceros beetle named Megalon.

PARIS HILTON
BIRTHDAY: FEBRUARY 17, 1981
BORN IN: NEW YORK, NEW YORK
ZODIAC SIGN: AQUARIUS
"BUT [ADHD] ALSO MAKES ME WHO I AM, SO IF I'M GOING TO LOVE MY LIFE, I HAVE TO LOVE MY ADHD. AND I DO LOVE MY LIFE."

As the great-granddaughter of the founder of Hilton Hotels, Paris Hilton has made a name for herself as a reality TV star, business-woman, philanthropist, and socialite.

Growing up between New York and Los Angeles, Paris first gained widespread attention when she co-starred with Nicole Richie in *The Simple Life*.

Although she was born with a LOT of financial privilege, Paris also has ADHD, and she's been open about how her ADHD affects her life and how she uses it in her day-to-day.

Paris has expanded into various business ventures, including fashion design, perfume, and music. She's also one of the world's highest-paid DJs and has launched a billion-dollar global retail and product empire.

After losing her home in the Palisades Fire in 2025, she quickly got on the ground to help other fire victims and even took in some foster dogs. She's a huge animal lover.

Today, Paris continues to inspire fans with her talent, resilience, and positive attitude.

Paris is obsessed with cereal and particularly loves eating Lucky Charms.

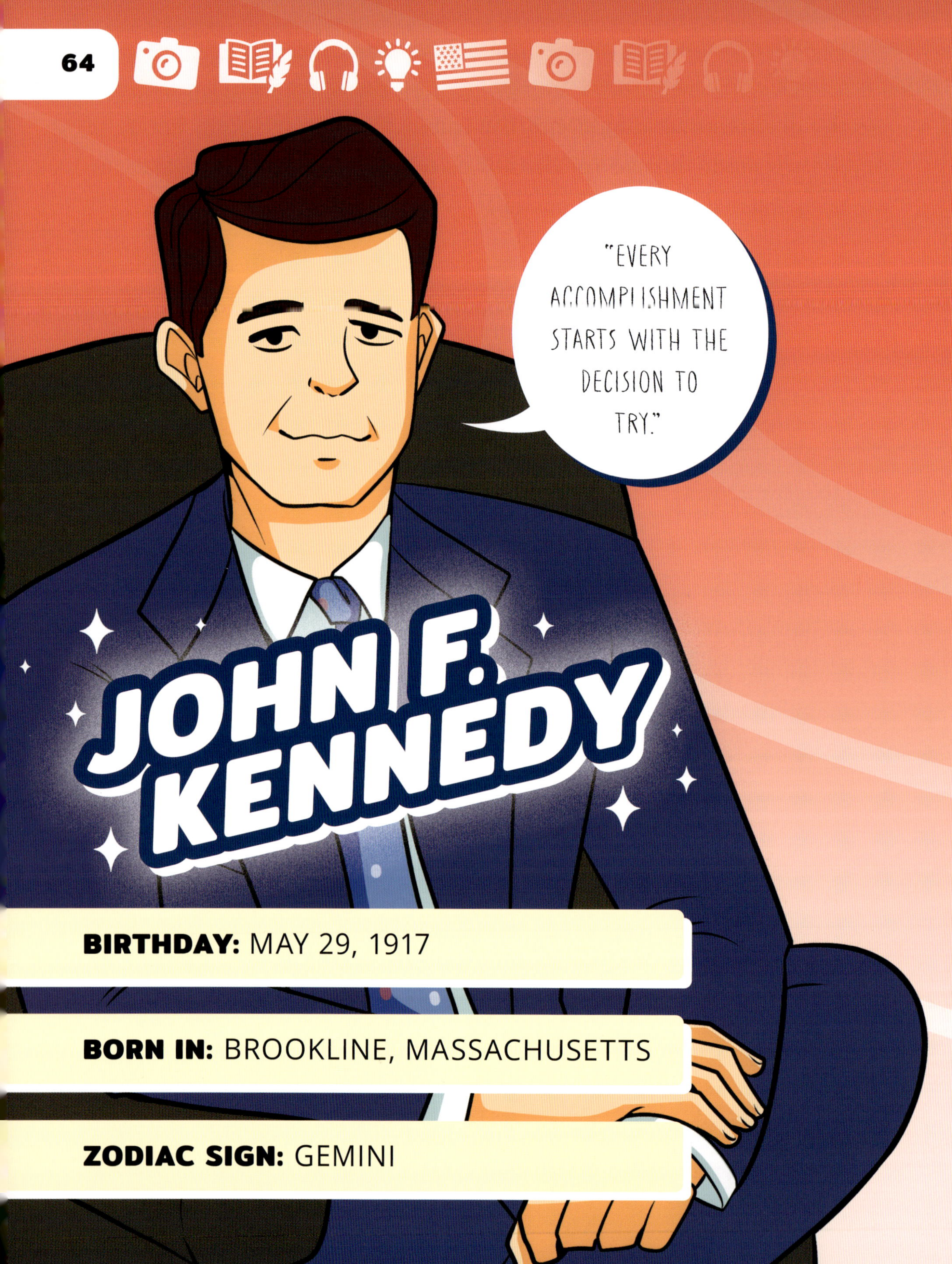

BIRTHDAY: MAY 29, 1917

BORN IN: BROOKLINE, MASSACHUSETTS

ZODIAC SIGN: GEMINI

John F. Kennedy, or JFK, was the thirty-fifth president of the United States. He was famous for being the youngest president elected (at age forty-three), and for his leadership during the Cuban Missile Crisis, as well as his vision for the space program and his focus on civil rights and social justice.

Though official diagnoses wouldn't pop up until after his death, JFK reportedly had difficulty focusing and concentrating, especially in school. He was known for his restless energy and impulsivity, traits often associated with ADHD.

Former United States Secretary of Commerce W. Averell Harriman wrote of the president: "He liked madcap drives to get to an airplane or dinner on time. He hated to waste time; in the morning he would read a magazine while taking a bath and at the same time shave there. . . . He was too much in a hurry, that he was going too far too fast, that he should pace himself better, that he should learn to take a breather. But the dynamo would not or could not slow down. He was always in the process of going or coming."

Despite his challenges, JFK's relentless drive and dynamic personality left an indelible mark on American history. His ability to inspire and lead, even in the face of personal struggles, continues to be remembered and celebrated today.

FUN FACT:

JFK liked to doodle sailboats in his spare time.

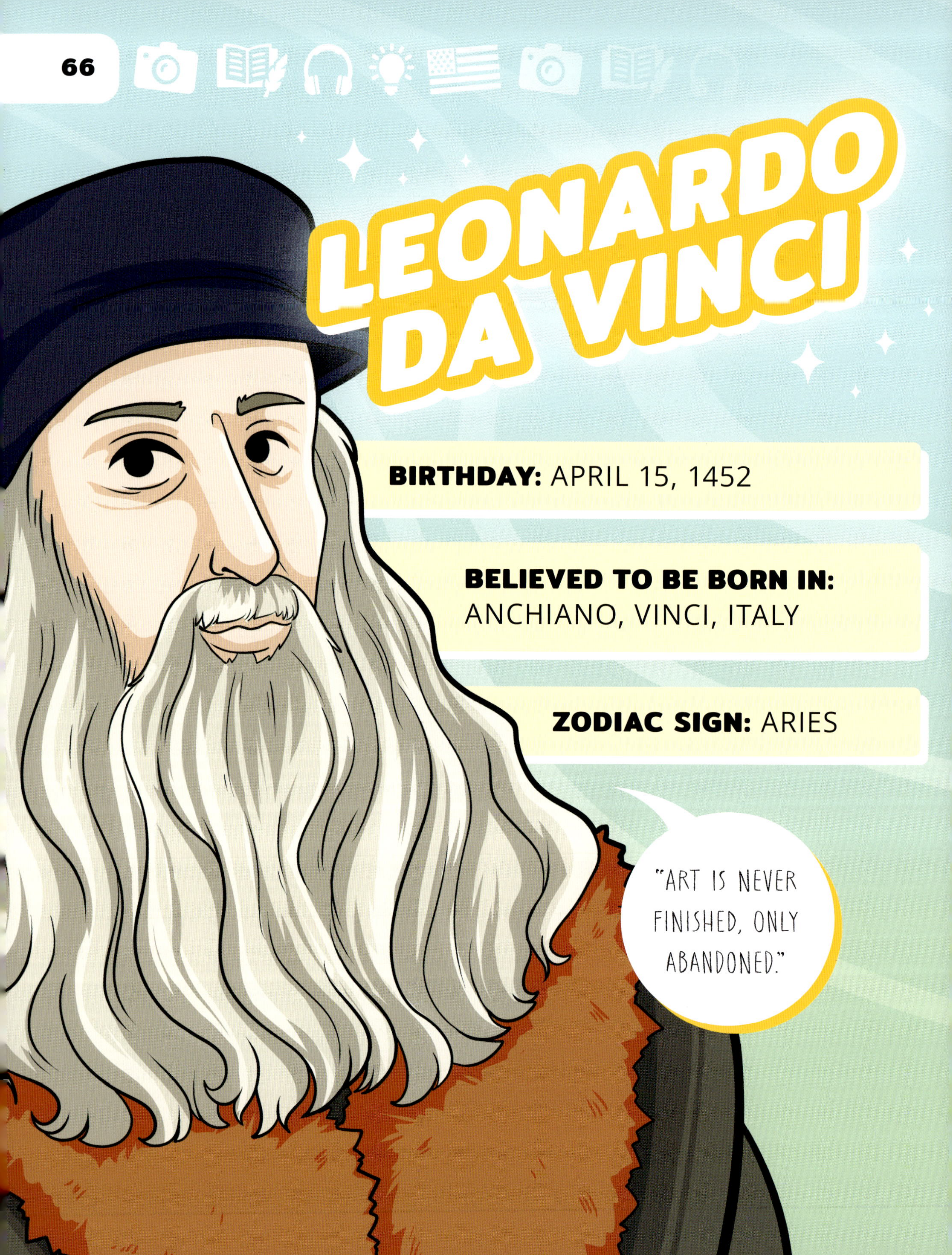
LEONARDO DA VINCI
BIRTHDAY: APRIL 15, 1452
BELIEVED TO BE BORN IN: ANCHIANO, VINCI, ITALY
ZODIAC SIGN: ARIES
"ART IS NEVER FINISHED, ONLY ABANDONED."

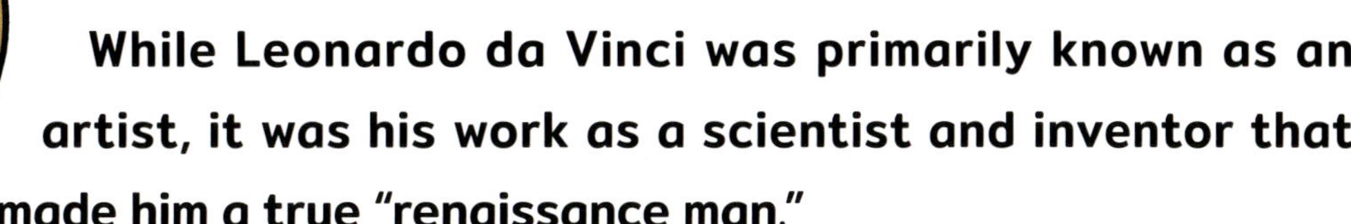

While Leonardo da Vinci was primarily known as an artist, it was his work as a scientist and inventor that made him a true "renaissance man."

Born Leonardo di ser Piero da Vinci, not much is known about the famous Italian changemaker's childhood. But that's okay, because we have plenty to celebrate Leonardo for in his adulthood.

In 1478, Leonardo was commissioned to paint an altarpiece for the Palazzo Vecchio in Florence, Italy. Three years later, he was commissioned to paint *The Adoration of the Magi*.

However, Leonardo finished neither project. Perhaps it was that classic ADHD inability to stay still, because he ended up abandoning the painting to provide services such as engineering design and music to the Duke of Milan.

Beyond painting masterpieces like *The Last Supper* and *Mona Lisa*, Leonardo also designed flying machines, drew detailed maps, studied the human body with startling accuracy, and even conceptualized early versions of tanks and robots.

While it's impossible to diagnose someone long after they're gone, Leonardo's biographers have noted that it is highly likely he had ADHD.

FUN FACT:

In 1994, Microsoft founder Bill Gates bought one of Leonardo's notebooks, the Codex Leicester, for $30,802,500—making it the most expensive manuscript ever sold at the time!

INSPIRED YET?

Now that you've met all these incredible people—writers, leaders, actors, athletes, and creators—you've seen something that they all have in common: ADHD didn't stop them from shining. In fact, it helped them think differently, dream big, and do things their own way.

Hopefully the stories of the people in this book help you to remember that ADHD brains might work differently, but that doesn't mean they're broken. It just means they're different. They're not neurotypical. They might need to try different tools, routines, or tricks to help them focus, but they can do amazing things, just like the stars in this book.

ABOUT THE AUTHOR

Wow, Terrance has never had an "About the Author" page before, despite writing dozens of books for popular brands like *Harry Potter*, *Fast and Furious*, *Afro Unicorn*, and *Piggy*.

He was diagnosed with ADHD when he was seven and took fifty-four milligram medications every morning with breakfast until he was fifteen.

Rumor has it he's still trying to find his attention to this day.

ABOUT THE ILLUSTRATOR

Rachel Cash is a digital artist from Burbank, California, living with her partner and their cat, Fio.

She's worked for the indie video game developer Colorgrave, doing character design and promotional art. She has also done designs for *The Last Unicorn*'s official merchandise and recently was co-illustrator on *Neopets: The Official Colouring Book*.

In Rachel's free time, she loves playing classics on her Gamecube like *Harvest Moon* and *Paper Mario*, or trying to find the best matcha in Los Angeles.